The art of war

Sun Tzu

Translation by Ethan Yet

Table of Contents

Preface

This is the world's first complete English translation of "The Art of War" and the most accurate English translation in the world.

About 512 BC, Sun Tzu wrote "The Art of War" and dedicated it to the king Helu. In 506 BC, Sun Tzu led the army of the Wu Kingdom with 30,000 troops to defeat the army of the Chu Kingdom with 200,000 troops, and captured the capital of Chu, Ying city, forcing King Zhao of Chu to flee. This war shocked the whole world because, at that time, the most powerful country in the world was the Chu. After that, the thirteen chapters of "The Art of War" began to influence the wars in Chinese history.

In 1772, "The Art of War" was translated into French by missionaries, and a book of military theory that had influenced China for more than two thousand years was officially introduced into the Western world. In 1910, Lionel Giles translated the first English version of "The Art of War". Until today, there are as many as twenty or thirty English translation versions. Among them, the one that best conveys the original meaning of "The Art of War" belongs to the version translated by Samuel B. Griffith in 1963. However, even with this version, the true meaning of the "The Art of War" that it can convey is actually only about 50%.

From this obvious objective fact, even if Napoleon had read "The Art of War", he might be affected by those wrong words; However, Liddell Hart, who once praised "The Art of War", has only about half of the knowledge of this book, including those wrong translations.

More importantly, no matter whether it is Napoleon or Liddell Hart, their correct understanding of "The Art of War" will not exceed 50%, which means that for the Western world, there are about 50% of the treasures of this book to be explored!

So from 1963 to the present, why are so many translators unable to translate a better version? And why does my version come close to fully expressing the ideas of "The Art of War"? What are the problems with those versions, so that the task of translating "The Art of War" can not be achieved completely and correctly!

There are many reasons why the previous translator could not translate "The Art of War" very well. In the period of missionaries and even Lionel Giles, Chinese culture was still not well understood, and modern Chinese is still in the development stage, and it is still immature. Therefore, these translators can only do almost direct translations of ancient languages.

In this way, whether the translator can translate correctly depends entirely on the translator's mastery and understanding of this ancient language. In ancient Chinese, due to language development, there were many polysemous words, and this knowledge was not at the hands of the missionaries and later scholars.

In addition, the translators of this period were not experts in military theory, and they lacked certain knowledge of the military field. Therefore, they cannot do translation work well. In the end, most sentences in the original text that are difficult for contemporary Chinese to understand are directly omitted without translation. And some vocabulary has also been translated into a mess, far from the original meaning of Sun Tzu!

Samuel is a general, so his understanding of military theory allows him to better master the work of translating "The Art of War". But the important reason why he can only correctly translate about 50% is that the Chinese version he is based on is problematic. These problems include that the version he is based on has many errors of character, followed by It is those words without errors that have misled Samuel's translation work because of wrong interpretations and annotations in the past. And Samuel and the translators after him are unable to solve the problems even realized, the reason is that the versions they are based on are not very different.

In 1972, archaeologists discovered the ancient version of "The Art of War" in the Han dynasty of Yinque Mountain in China. This version is the early version of the Han Dynasty. Although its appearance has solved many of the problems that have always been disputed by annotators. But the remaining problems are still many.

In 1999, I spent more than a decade to study "The Art of War". During this time, I collected all relevant documents from the Spring and Autumn Period of "The Art of War" to the Song Dynasty, including quotations and notes, and then used philology, linguistics, logic, and military theory. The restoration of the original text of "The Art of War", as well as the dialectical work on the differences in the annotations of the past generations Controversy between different annotators about a sentence that contradicts each other. This version has, therefore, become the most accurate version of the contemporary era. Almost all the problems in the text and translation of "The Art of War" have been solved in my one-million-word book "A thorough study of Sun Tzu's art of war".

Later, it took me nearly five years to translate this classic into modern Chinese. This English translation is based on this Chinese translation.

My translation is more accurate than other versions and can convey the original intention of Sun Tzu. It is also more complete than all versions. It is also the only complete translation that does not miss any sentence. Since I have made statistics on the rhetorical style of "The Art of War", and know that this is an important component of the "The Art of War", I hope to keep the same rhetorical style in the English version as much as possible! Because Sun Tzu uses the same rhetorical style in "The Art of War", it usually means that these sentences with the same rhetorical style are in the same category. Therefore, retaining this rhetorical style will undoubtedly help readers understand the original text.

Secondly, Sun Tzu used ancient Chinese for creation, but the language has continued to evolve from ancient times to today. Therefore, this will cause several things to happen. First, some concepts discovered by Sun Tzu at that time have more precise names today, and second, because Chinese itself is a hieroglyph and the vocabulary is composed of characters, some concepts are easy to associate with people who understand Chinese But it's different for people who don't understand Chinese.

For example, the word "天(tian)" originally meant "sky", and it can derive the concept of "weather and climate". In English, the hypernym that summarizes the concept of "weather and climate" is the concept of "meteorology". Although this concept is a term that came into being in modern times, and it covers a wider range, it is undoubtedly the concept that Sun Tzu wants to express. It was just that there was no corresponding vocabulary at that time! So when the translator translates the word into "sky" or even " heaven ", it has nothing to do with what the Sun Tzu wants to say! For a general, how should he master the rules of "sky" or even "heaven"?

I thought deeply about where Sun Tzu used what kind of vocabulary and the precise correspondence between ancient concepts and contemporary vocabulary. The translation of "tian" is just one example.

Therefore, compared with other contemporary translations, this translation has the following characteristics:

1. Completely convey the idea of "The Art of War". It solves the problem of simplified translation, rewriting or even non-translation that is commonly used in many current translations because the translator does not understand the original text.

2. Solved the problem of typographical errors in the original text.

3. Solve the problem of the misunderstanding of the original text by the annotators and translators of previous generations.

4. Solved the conceptual correspondence between many ancient Chinese and contemporary English.

5. The rhetorical style used in as many original texts as possible is retained.

6. Many contemporary translations lack the understanding of "The Art of War" and philosophy, so they often translated the highly abstract concepts of Sun Tzu concretely. A practical example to cover higher-level abstract concepts, such as using a white horse to refer to all Horse. And this is undoubtedly a retrogression of thought. And our translation also solves this problem that is ubiquitous in many translations but few people realize.

Of course, this translation is not without defects. After all, English is not my native language, and in order to preserve Sun Tzu's original rhetorical style as much as possible, the translation of many sentences may be closer to the thinking mode of Chinese speakers than English speakers.

Although this "The Art of War" translation is not the first English translation, nor the most well-written of all, it is undoubtedly the first truly complete and accurate translation of Sun Tzu's thoughts. I have put a lot of effort into the translation of this classic, and I also hope that this translation will allow readers in the Western world to re-understand Sun Tzu and his "The Art of War".

Ethan Yet 2020.4.13

About the author

Sun Tzu is also known as Sun Wu, a native of Qi, and lived in the late Spring and Autumn period. It is China's greatest military thinker!

Sun Tzu was mainly active from 524 BC to 506 BC. In 511 BC, Confucius received funding from Lu Zhao Gong, the monarch of the Lu state, and went to the royal family of the Zhou Dynasty to learn etiquette from Laozi, who was then the director of the royal library. So these three great men who have influenced China for thousands of years in the field of thought are actually living in the same era.

As far as Sun Tzu 's life is concerned, all he can know at the moment is the details of his writing of "The Art of War" in 512 BC, and that he followed king Helu and prime minister Wu Zixu to attack Chu in 506 BC.

Sun Tzu 's fame, and "The Art of War" have been handed down to today, which is related to his record of many wars against the Chu. His greatest record was that he led Wu 's army of 30,000 troops to defeat Chu 's 200,000 troops. At that time, the Chu state's military strength was probably more than one million, but except for those 200,000 troops, other armies had little chance to be organized against the army of Wu.

After Sun Tzu joined the Wu Kingdom, Wu's army was divided into three parts. Every time Sun Tzu used one of three troops to attack the border cities of Chu. After the Chu assembled the troops from other places, Wu's troops retreat back to Wu. After the troops assembled in the Chu retreated, Sun Tzu sent another troop to continue attacking the Chu. Do this loop operation. Eventually, in about six years, the Chu army and the people were exhausted, and the Wu army received additional training from these operations, and the soldiers were more familiar with the Chu terrain. All these brought great benefits to the whole army led by Sun Tzu to attack the Kingdom of Chu.

506 BC. The monarchs of Cai and Tang were finally released after being imprisoned by the prime minister of Chu for several years. The monarchs of both countries, therefore, wanted revenge. Sun Tzu thought that the time to attack the Chu was ripe, so the army that united Cai and Tang began to invade the Chu. Sun Tzu did not attack all the cities along the way from the border of Chu, but bypassed many cities and directly hit the capital of Chu. Due to the marching speed of the army, the Chu army is

not as powerful as the Wu army, and even if it has a numerical advantage, it is still defeated. Eventually, the prime minister who led the Chu army committed suicide, and King Chu Zhao of the Chu Kingdom fled from the capital in panic. Wu almost unified the Chu! Although later the Wu army had to retreat back to Wu because of many failed decisions by King Helu. But this battle also shocked the world! And Sun Tzu and "The Art of War" are also well known! "The Art of War" has influenced almost every war in China since then!

Calculations before the war

Sun Tzu said:

War is a major event for the country! It has a bearing on the lives and deaths of the people and the survival of the country. It must be studied clearly!

Therefore, five things are used as the general administrative program, and the state of these five things is used as the direction of comparison between the enemy and us to explore the true situation of each other's strength. One is called the Tao, the second is called the Meteorology, the third is called the Terrain, the fourth is called the General, and the fifth is called the Law.

"Tao"[1] means: people and the superior have the same will so that the superior can go through fire and water with the people, and the people will not betray him!

"Meteorology" refers to the cloudy(Yin)[2] and sunny(Yang)[3] of the weather, and the cold and heat of the climate and their changes are controlled by time.

"Terrain" refers to the five relative properties of "high and low, wide and narrow, far and near, steep and flat, dangerous and safe."

"General" means: the general needs to possess five virtues: " wisdom, credit, benevolence, courage, and strictness."

---

[1] "Tao" has multiple meanings in ancient Chinese, such as road, method, rule and even moral. As far as Sun Tzu is concerned, it is more "moral", but not completely equivalent. There is no corresponding concept in English, so transliteration is adopted.

[2] "Yin" refers to everything dark and cold. So in terms of weather conditions, it is cloudy.

[3] "Yang" refers to everything bright and hot. So in terms of weather conditions, it is sunny.

"Law" refers to three methods: the establishment system of the army (organization), the command mode of the officials (management), and the use of the monarch (decision making). All these five things have been heard by the general; He who knows the truth can win, and He who does not know the truth cannot win.

Therefore, several issues should be used as the direction of comparison between the enemy and us to explore the true situation of each other's strength. These things are: whose monarch is wiser? Whose generals are more capable? Who gets the right time and benefits of terrain? Whose statute has been followed? Whose army is stronger? Whose soldiers are better trained? Whose rewards and punishments are fair? With these comparative data, I can know who will win and who will lose!

If the general follows my calculations, and he will surely win the battle, then retain him; If the general does not follow my calculations, he will definitely lose the battle, then dismiss him.

The result of the calculation is favorable and obeyed by the general, so the monarch could build up general's reputation and establish general's majesty, so that general can get help when fighting with troops. How much authority should be established for the general, this is determined by how much benefit this war will bring!

Military action is a violation of the norm!

Therefore, if we have the ability then show the enemy that we don't have that if we have used something then show the enemy that we have not use it.

When we are close to the enemy, we show that we are far away, and when we are far from the enemy, we show that we are close.

Our army deliberately abandoned some benefits to seduce the enemy. Our army deliberately disrupted its formation to seduce the enemy to attack. Our army was strong but deliberately prepared for the enemy. Our army was powerful but deliberately avoided the enemy. Our army was angered but deliberately adopt a strategy of watching the enemy; (after the enemy is taken lightly) and attack the enemy when he is unprepared, and take actions beyond his expectations. These are the methods that the generals use to win. Those should not be revealed in advance!

Before the battle, we compared the strength of the enemy and ours in the temple. The calculation result is better than the enemy, we get more chips; the calculation result is not better than the enemy, we get less chips. More chips have a higher chance of winning, and less chips have a higher chance of failure, not to mention that there are no chips! I use this method to observe the war, then the victory and defeat have already appeared!

Process of war

Sun Tzu said:

The process of preparing for war is that war requires about 1,000 light fighting vehicles, 1,000 leather vehicles and a troop of 100,000 heavily armed soldiers. If the grain is to be transported to battlefields that are thousands of miles away, there will be the cost of domestic and foreign funds, the expenses of the staff, the money to buy the materials needed to repair the chariot, and the salaries for soldiers and chariot warriors. All the above add up to 1,000 taels of gold a day, and then the dispatch of 100,000 troops is completed.

Fighting with these 100,000 troops takes a long time to win, then the soldier's agility will be dull and the weapon's sharpness will be damaged. If they attack a castle, their strength will suffer a great loss. If the army stays abroad for a long time, the country's funds will be insufficient.

If a country has the situation of "unagile army, sharp damage to weapons, loss of military strength, and depletion of country's funds", then other countries will attack him when these disadvantages occur. If a country encounters such a situation, even the wise cannot deal with it!

Therefore, in military operations, there are only heard about people pursuing quick victory with simple tactics but never seen people pursuing slow victory with clever tactics. There is never a long war beneficial to the country.

Therefore, the benefits of fighting can't be obtained if the harm of fighting is not fully understood.

Therefore, for those who are good at using troops, the army no longer conscripts for a second time, and the food is no longer transported a second time; weapons and equipment are obtained from the country, and food is replenished from the enemy, so his army's food can reach a sufficient state!

The reason why the country leads to poverty due to war is because of the need for long-distance material transportation to the expeditionary army, and long-distance material transportation will make the people poor; near the army, the price of materials there will also soar. The soaring prices of materials will cause domestic people to pay more taxes to support the expenditure of the army; more taxes paid by the people will exhaust their financial resources, and exhausting their financial resources will cause them The urge to work to support life and expenses.

After such a war, the strength of the army was lost on the battlefield, and the homes of the people in the country were emptied, and 60% of the war cost paid by the people will be lost.

The public equipment was also severely damaged. In return were broken chariots and tired horses. Meanwhile, Armor, bows, arrows, crossbows, halberds, shields, spears, various weapons and equipment, and Cattle and big cars for carrying supplies also went to lost 70%.

Therefore, a wise general must be committed to obtaining food from the enemy, eating 1 liter of the enemy's food is worth 200 liters of his own food; using 1 liter of the fodder of the enemy (for feeding cattle and horses) is worth using his own forage 20 liters.

Therefore, the soldiers were brave enough to kill the enemy, because it was full of anger; the soldiers seize the enemy's goods because it is profitable!

During the battle of vehicle: when soldiers get more than ten enemy chariots, they will reward the one who gets the first one, and change the banner of the chariot. The mixed-use of the acquired chariots, and the scattered use of the surrendered soldiers, is called defeating the enemy but becoming stronger.

So military operations value speed rather than endurance.

Therefore, the general who knows the laws of the military is like the god of life who controls the lives of the people. At the same time, he is also the master who determines whether the country is safe or dangerous!

Use strategy to attack

Sun Tzu said:

The method of using army: The one who wins and the country remains intact is brilliant, the one who wins and the country is damaged is second-class.

The one who wins and the army remains intact is brilliant, the one who wins and the army is damaged is second-class.

The one who wins and the brigade units remain intact is brilliant, the one who wins and the brigade units are damaged is second-class.

The one who wins and the army squad remains intact is brilliant, the one who wins and the army squad is damaged is second-class.

Therefore, winning one hundred victories in one hundred battles is not the most brilliant. Winning victory without fighting is the most brilliant.

So the best strategy of using power is to use strategy, followed by diplomatic means, followed by the use of military operations, and the lowest strategy is to attack enemy castles.

The process of attacking the castle: It takes three months to prepare the siege equipment such as super-sized shields and siege engines; it takes another three months to complete the construction of the battering ram and siege mound!

During the siege, the general was unable to overcome the anger in his heart, and he orders his troops to climb the wall like ants; therefore, he lost a third of the soldiers and the castle was still not captured. This is a disaster caused by the siege!

Therefore, a general who is good at using the army, subdues the enemy's army without fighting, captures the enemy 's castles without using siege methods, and destroys the enemy's country without taking too long. He will fight for the world with a strategy that will keep his power intact so that his weapons will remain intact and his interests intact. This is how to use strategy as a means of attack.

The method of using army: soldiers ten times as many as the enemy will surround him, five times as many as the enemy will directly attack him, twice as many as the enemy will disperse his forces, the number of equal will be able to defeat him, less than the enemy will be able to defend him, not as many as the enemy will be able to temporarily avoid him. If the general follows these rules, then even if the army is smaller than the enemy, the defense can still be strong; If the army is larger than the enemy, it can capture the enemy.

The general is an important assistant to the country! The more comprehensive the general assists the country, the stronger the country will be; the less a general helps a country, the weaker it becomes.

What makes a monarch a danger to an army is mainly manifested in three aspects: The first is that he does not know that the army cannot move forward, but orders them to advance; he does not know that the army cannot retreat but orders them to retreat. It is called a fettered army. The second is that if he does not understand the affairs in the army, but participate in the military's decree, then the officers and soldiers of the army will be confused! The third is that if he does not know the mission of the army, but participate in the decision-making of the army, then officers and soldiers of the army will doubt it! If officers and soldiers are both confused and doubtful, then the day is coming for other vassals to bring disaster to this country! This situation is called disrupting your military to attract the enemy to win!

Therefore, there are five elements that make the army more likely to win: 1, know when to fight and when not to fight, win the odds. 2. Those who know how to use a large number of troops and a small number of troops, win the odds. 3. The superior and the inferior have the same idea, win the odds. 4, with an alert mindset to deal with unguarded enemies, win the odds. 5, if the general has the ability and the monarch does not control him, win the odds. These five items are the way to make yourself a winner!

Therefore, in the war, those who understand the enemy and themselves, even if they fight a hundred times, there is no danger; those who understand themselves but not the enemy have half a chance to win and half a chance to fail; those who do not understand the enemy and themselves will be in danger in every battle.

Form

Sun Tzu said:

An ancient master of the military, he first makes himself can not be defeated and then waits for an opportunity of defeating the enemy. That we can be defeated by the enemy lies in our own hands, but the opportunity of defeating the enemy is provided by the enemy himself.

Therefore, the master of the military who can make himself not defeated by the enemy, but cannot make the enemy be defeated. So, victory can be predicted, but not manipulated.

When the enemy cannot be defeated, we adopt a defensive strategy; when he can be defeated, we adopt an offensive strategy.

The use of defensive strategy can let your power to save and appear more than enough; The use of offensive strategy, will make your own power loss and appear insufficient.

The ancient masters of defense, who hid their armies in unpredictable places, and when they attacked, they were as unexpected as if they had flown from heaven. So they can keep themselves intact and win!

Foreseeing victory is just what most people know. This is not a brilliant man; fighting to win, and everyone in the world says he is clever. This is not really a brilliant man!

Therefore, lifting a hair is not considered to be very powerful in strength, seeing the sun and the moon is not considered to be excellent in eyesight, and hearing thunder is not considered to be sensitive in hearing.

So the so-called brilliant man is that who defeated the enemy who is easily defeated!

A brilliant man, therefore, will have no strange victories, no reputation for wisdom, no achievement for bravery, as a result of his battles.

He won't encounter danger when he wins. The reason why he won't encounter danger is that his strategy to win is used to win enemies who have already failed!

Therefore, a brilliant person first stands in a position that cannot be defeated without losing the opportunity to defeat the enemy.

Therefore, the victorious army wins before it fights, and the defeated army fights before it seeks victory.

Therefore, the master of the military, following the rules mentioned above and keeping the rules listed below, can be the lord of victory.

To know where the battlefield is, you can measure the battlefield space between you and enemy, then you can estimate how many troops can be placed in that space, then you can calculate the number of soldiers that may participate in each other, Then you can compare the strength of each other, then you can predict who will win.

So a victorious army, fighting the enemy, is like using Yi to compare weight with Ju[4]; A defeated army, fighting its enemies, is like using Ju to compare weight with Yi.

The heavier side, he used soldiers to fight, as if it was to crack from a crack on a levee a thousand feet high and filled with water. This effect is caused by the gap of "form"!

---

[4] Yi and Ju are also ancient weights. Sun Tzu's original analogy used two weights that differed greatly in weight, one called Yi and one called Ju. Twenty-four Ju is equal to one tael, twenty-four tael is equal to one Yi, so one Yi is equal to five hundred and seventy-six Ju. One tael at the time equaled 15.8 grams. The metaphor uses the very heavy against the very light, which means there is a big gap between the two forces. Because there is no corresponding concept in English, so I use transliteration here.

Position

Sun Tzu said:

Managing "a large number of troops" is like managing "a small number of troops". This is because the army is divided into several units for hierarchical management!

Fighting with "large numbers of troops" is like fighting with "small numbers of troops". This is because of the good use of visual and auditory command tools!

Putting a large number of troops into battle can make them withstand enemy attacks without being defeated. This is because of the use of peculiar and positive tactics![5]

The force exerted by the army on the enemy is like throwing a whetstone on an egg. This is because of the use of full and hollow tactics![6]

The method of battle is using positive troops to fight and using the peculiar troops to win.

---

[5] "Peculiar(奇, qi) and Positive(正, zheng)" is the term Sun Tzu introduced into military theory. "Positive" has normal, regular, visible and knowable meanings, and " Peculiar " has abnormal, irregular, invisible and unknowable meanings. In real use, " Peculiar troops" can be included in "Positive troops", but it uses completely opposite or different signals to control, in order to achieve unexpected effects of the enemy. Normally, the two forces are used separately.

[6] "Full(實, shr)and Hollow(虛, syu)" is the term Sun Tzu introduced into military theory. "Full" has the meaning of fullness, firmness, truth and real. "Hollow" has the meaning of empty, soft, false and illusory.

Therefore, those who are good at using peculiar soldiers, his peculiar soldiers are as endless as heaven and earth, as if the Yellow River and the sea are not dry up.

When it is over, it starts again, like the alternation of the sun and the moon; when it dies, it is born again, like the cycle of the four seasons.

The sound is only five basic tones, but after the free combination of these five tones, they cannot be heard through. The colors are only five basic hues, but after the free combination of these five hues, they cannot be seen through. The taste is only five basic flavors, but after the free combination of these five flavors, they cannot be taste through! The fighting position is only two basic states of "peculiar" and "positive". However, after the free combination of "peculiar" and "positive", they cannot be exhausted!

The process of transforming and applying between peculiar and positive troops is like a circle with no end to find. Who can exhaust it?

The water is rushing so fast that it can float the stone. This is because the "position" plays a role in it; the fierce birds attacking the prey can cause a state of destruction, which is the effect of "distance ". Therefore, the person who is good at combating is in a dangerous position, and his distance between him and the enemy is short; his position is like a crossbow machine pulled out, and the distance between him and the enemy is like the distance between his finger and the trigger.

He has a seemingly chaotic formation, but attacking with such a seemingly chaotic army will not be really chaotic; he has a seemingly billowing formation, although its shape looks round, It will not be defeated.

The disorder is transformed from order, timidity is transformed from courage, and weakness is transformed from strength. Order and disorder are caused by changes in tactics; bravery and timidity are caused by the gap of potential; strength and weakness are caused by the difference of physical forms.

The man who is good at mobilizing the enemy: he gives the enemy an illusion, and the enemy must chase it; he gives the enemy a bait, and the enemy must fight for it. Use the positive troops to mobilize the enemy, and the peculiar troops to wait for the enemy.

Therefore, those who are good at fighting, seek the conditions of victory in the position of the enemy and us and do not blame the soldiers for their best efforts, so they can release the soldiers and depend on the position to win.

The man who depends on the position, he uses soldiers to fight as if turning wood and stones. The characteristics of wood and stone are: when it is stable, it is stationary, when it is dangerous, it moves; when it is square, it does not move, and when it is round, it does not stop.

Therefore, the man who is good at fighting, he uses soldiers to fight, as if turning a round stone on a mountain that is thousands of miles high. This effect is caused by the difference in "position"!

Full and Hollow tactics

Sun Tzu said:

Those who arrive earlier at the battle site to wait for battle have the advantage of ease; those who arrive later at the battle site and rush to war have the disadvantage of fatigue. So those who are good at fighting, mobilize the enemy without being mobilized by the enemy.

We can make the enemy come to the battlefield on our own because we make him think that it is "good" for him to do so; we can make the enemy not because we make him think that it is "harmful" to him!

We can make the enemy who is at ease wearies, and the enemy who is at well-fed hungry, this is because we appear in the place where he must rush to rescue. The soldiers walk thousands of miles without fear, this is because they are walking on a road that will not encounter the enemy.

The attack is sure to win, this is because the attack is where the enemy does not defend! The defense is sure to be strong. This is because the defense is where the enemy is sure to attack! So those who are good at attacking let the enemy does not know where to defend; those who are good at defending let the enemy does not know where to attack!

Tiny and tiny! Bring the army to a state of no form! Amazing and amazing! Bring the army to a state of no sound! When the army reaches this level, it can become the lord of the enemy's life.

If we attack and the enemy cannot fight with us, that is because we strike at the enemy's weakness; Our retreat was unstoppable by the enemy, that is because we were too far away to catch up.

If we want to fight, even though the enemy had built a high camp and dug a deep trench and wants to hold on, he still has to fight with us. This is because we are attacking where he must go to rescue. If we do not want to fight. Even if we only draw a line on the ground to defend, the enemy is still unable to fight with us. This is because we have left the place where he attacked!

Therefore, those who are good at commanding the army can make the enemy appear in form and make their own form disappear (invisible), then our forces can be concentrated, and the enemy's forces will be dispersed. Our concentration became one, and the enemy dispersed into ten parts, which allowed us to attack the enemy with ten times the force of the enemy!

When we are small and the enemy is large, if we want to defeat a large army with a small army, we cannot let the enemy know where we are going to attack. If the enemy does not know where we are going to attack, the enemy has more places to defend against. The more places the enemy has to defend, the fewer men he can fight!

So guarding the people in front will reduce the strength behind him; guarding the people behind will reduce the strength in front of him; guarding the people on the left will reduce the strength on his right; guarding the people on the right will reduce the strength on his left. There is no place where he is not guarded, and there is no place where his forces are not small.

Therefore, a small number of troops are due to our defense of the enemy in many places; a large number of troops are caused by the enemy defending us in many places.

If you know the date of the war and the location of the war, you can go to war even if the battlefield is thousands of miles away. If you don't know the date of the war and the location of the war, even if the troops at the front can't rescue the troops at the back, the troops at the back can't rescue the troops at the front, the troops at the left can't rescue the troops at the right, the troops at the right can't rescue the troops at the left.

Let alone, the distance between the troops which the far one is dozens of miles away, and the near one is also miles away!

Therefore, according to my calculations, although there are a lot more troops than the enemy, what help can it have for winning?

So saying: victory can be monopolized; although the number of enemies is large, we can make them unable to fight us!

Therefore, the method of reconnaissance is used to learn the rules of movement between the enemy and ourselves, the method of manifesting the form is used to know that it is currently in a dangerous or safe situation, the method of calculation is used to learn the gains and losses of the strategy, and the method of comparison is used to know where the army is capable or not.

The ultimate change in military form is no form. An army has no form, so even a deep spy cannot peep at it, and even a wise man cannot plot it.

Relying on the form to develop a strategy to win everyone, everyone can not understand the mystery, people only know the form I use to win, but do not know the principle I use to formulate a winning form. Therefore, after the victory, you should not persist in reusing the same form. Instead, you should always change your form by the enemy's form.

The form of the army is like water: When the water is flowing, avoid the high and tend to the low; the army's winning tactics, avoid the solid enemy and attack the weak one. The water depends on the terrain to formulate the direction of flow, and the army depends on the enemy to formulate a winning strategy.

Letting the army have no fixed position, no fixed form, and can change with the enemy, this is called reaching a magical realm.

(It's like) There is no permanent winner among the five elements, and there is no season in the four seasons that can occupy time forever. The hours of sunlight are sometimes long and sometimes short, and the shape of the moon is sometimes full and sometimes deficient. (Everything is changing.)

Use the army to compete

Sun Tzu said:

The rule of using soldiers: the general accepts the order of the monarch, joins the army, gathers the soldiers, and completes the camp to allow the army to rest. These actions are not as difficult as the enemy and us competing for a certain goal.

The difficulty for the enemy and our army to compete with each other is that the generals must be able to turn the tortuous path into a straight path and turn disasters into benefits. Therefore, the people who can make our marching path tortuous, to paralyze the enemy, and lure him with benefits to hinder their actions, and thus can set out later and arrive first, know how to use the tortuous and straight strategy!

The enemy and our army compete with each other to gain interests and to resolve the crisis.

If we use the entire army to compete for interests, it will inevitably be unable to catch up with the enemy because of the slow speed.

If we abandon some slower troops and compete for interests, our army may lose equipment and food.

Therefore, if the commander ordered the soldiers to wear armor to chase the interests, it would make the army unable to get rest in the morning and night, and walk twice as much as usual.

If the army goes to a place a hundred miles away to compete for interests, then the superior general will also be arrested; the energetic soldier is in front, and the tired soldier is in the back, so only one of the ten soldiers can reach the destination! If the army goes to a place fifty miles away to compete for interests, then the top general will also fail, because only half of his army can reach his destination! If you go to a place thirty miles away to compete for interests, only two-thirds of the soldiers can reach their destination.

If the army does not have weapons and equipment, it will perish, without food, it will perish, and without energy and materials, it will perish. (So it's dangerous to go long distances to compete for interests.)

Therefore, if you do not know the plots of the vassals, you cannot associate with them in advance; you cannot march if you do not know the terrain such as mountains, forests, obstacles, and rivers; you cannot get geographical advantages without using the locals as a guide.

The army exists in the form of deception. Its action is decided by the advantage or not. It changes by dispersion and aggregation!

Therefore, when an army moves, its haste should be like the wind, its slowness should be like the forest, its aggression should be like the fire, its immobility should be like the mountain, its unpredictability should be like the overcast day, its action should be like the thunder.

Deciding the direction of advance, commanding decentralized operations, or allocating land for profit distribution should all be weighed against gains and losses before taking action. Anyone who knows how to use a tortuous and straight strategy will win. This is the way to compete with the army!

According to the book "military politics", "on the battlefield, we can't hear each other clearly, so we use" drum and gongs "; we can't see each other's movements clearly, so we use " flags". Therefore, more " flags" should be used in daytime operations, and more "drums and gongs " should be used in night operations. "Drum and gongs " and " flags " are used to unify the ears and eyes of the soldiers. Now that the way in which the soldiers received their orders had been unified, the brave could not move forward alone, and the timid could not move backward alone. This is the way to command a large number of troops.

Soldiers can be deprived of strength, generals can be deprived of mind.

The strength of the soldiers was sharp in the morning, and lazy in the daytime, and collapsed after dusk.

Therefore, those who are good at using troops: they avoid the enemy in a state of sharpness and attack the enemy in a state of laziness and collapse. This is the way to gain an advantage in "pneuma".

Using an orderly army to wait for chaotic enemy troops and a quiet army to wait for noisy enemy troops. These are the way to gain an advantage in "psychological ".

Waiting for the enemy farther away from the battlefield with the army closer to the battlefield, waiting for the fatigued enemy army with a stable and rested army, and waiting for the hungry enemy army with a well-fed army. These are the way to gain an advantage in " physical strength ".

Don't intercept the army who have a state of neat flags, and don't attack the army who have a strict and solemn formation. This is the way to gain an advantage in "expedient."

The law of using army: don't upwardly attack the enemy when they have occupied high ground, don't attack the decoy troops released by the enemy, don't force the enemy who has no retreat, don't attack the troops with sharp spirit, don't fight an army with its back to the hills, don't chase enemy forces who pretend to fail, surround the enemy and leave an outlet free, do not Intercept the enemy who is retreating back to his country from the front. This is the way of using the army!

Nine contingency measures

Sun Tzu said:

All the rules of using soldiers: the general accepts the order of the monarch, joins the army, gathers the soldiers, and camps.

(It must be noted afterward :) When the army is in the "lonely terrain", it cannot stay there. When the army on the "meeting terrain", his army should carry out joint operations with his allies. When the army in the "covered terrain", it should not camp overnight in the place. When the army is in the "enclosed terrain", it must be carefully planned. And when the army is in the "dead terrain", it must fight quickly.

Meanwhile, some roads should not go through, some enemy forces should not attack, some castle should not capture, some land should not scramble, some monarch's orders should not be obeyed!

Therefore, if the general can fully understand the benefits of the nine contingency measures, this means that he knows how to use the force. if the general can't fully understand the benefits of the nine contingency measures, then even if he knows the terrain, he cannot get the benefits provided by the terrain itself!

The general manages the army but does not know how to use these nine kinds of contingency measures, so although he knows the benefits of these nine kinds of contingency measures, he cannot get the best effect of manpower!

Therefore, the wise man must mix the "beneficial" and "harmful" aspects when he is thinking. Mixed with the beneficial side, so the purpose can be achieved; Mixed with the harmful side, so the scourge can be lifted.

Therefore (if you want to deal with the vassals), you can use the harm to subdue the vassals, use the achievements to control them, and use the interests to drive them.

So the law of war is: don't be confident that the enemy will not come, to be confident that I have the way to deal with the enemy. Do not be confident that the enemy not to attack us, but be confident that we have places where they can not attack.

Therefore, there are five dangers of being a general: the general who is determined to die must kill him, the general who is afraid of death can capture him, the general who is prone to anger can insult him, the general who is incorrupt can stigmatize and humiliate him, and the general who loves his people and his soldiers can bother him.

These five situations are the fault of the general and the disaster of using soldiers! The destruction of the army, the general was killed, must be because of these five dangers, so the general must study these five situations clearly!

Marching

Sun Tzu said:

As for the actions of the military on various space activities and the matters to be noticed when observing the actions of the enemy, there are mainly the following:

When the army crosses the mountains, it will walk along the valley. When deploying the army, the general should choose a place with a wide field of vision and a high terrain. When the enemy forces that charge from the top to the bottom, do not fight from the bottom to the top. These are the activity in What the army in the valley should pay attention to.

If the enemy is crossing the water, our army must temporarily leave the water, so that the enemy forces have no scruples. If the enemy is coming across the river, our army should not meet him at the water's edge. It would be better to attack after half the enemy has crossed the river.

If you want to fight against the enemy, don't attach the army to the river bank to face him. When the general deploys the army, it is advisable to choose a place with a wide field of vision and high terrain, and not to face the river. These are something that the army moving in the river zone should pay attention to.

The army must leave as soon as possible without stopping to avoid an ambush when passing through the swamp. If you engage the enemy in the swamp zone, you can let the army lean on the water grass and lean against the trees. These are what the army in the swamp zone should pay attention to.

When deploying the army on the plains and land, the general should choose a wide terrain, and the right side and the back of the army can best depend on the high ground. The army is facing the enemy in front of the army to facilitate the decisive battle; the road behind the army is clear to facilitate the supply.

These are what the army on land should pay attention to.

These four laws that benefit the army are the methods used by the Yellow Emperor to win the four emperors!

The soldiers like high places and dislike low places, and they pay attention to the places with Yang qi and despise the places with Yin qi. If the general can keep the army alive, and station the army in a solid place, this is called " the inevitable triumph over the environment ". Such an environment makes soldiers healthy without being infected with hundreds of diseases.

If an army is near a hill or dike, it must be stationed "south of the hill and north of the water," where there is plenty of sunshine, and the army must attach to it on the right and the back. This is good for the army, and it is also the help that the terrain gives the army.

There was heavy rain in the upper reaches of the big river, and the current had arrived; then stop wading through the river and wait for it to settle down before embarking on the crossing.

When the army passes by a mountain stream, if it encounters a vast and natural terrain like "water wells, cells, snares, traps, crevices", it must leave it as soon as possible, do not approach it! Keep our army away from it, make the enemy close to it; make our army face it, and make the enemy's back towards it.

There are dangerous obstacles and difficult roads, pools, and wells, reeds, bushes, weeds beside the army. All places that can be hidden and cover must be searched carefully and repeatedly. These are the places where the spies can hide!

The enemy is close to me and still able to keep quiet. This is because he takes advantage of the dangerous terrain; the enemy challenges us from a long distance and wants us to attack first, this is because he occupies a wide and flat and advantageous terrain!

The phenomenon that many trees are swaying, which means that the enemy is coming here; where there are many weeds and many obstructions, is worthy of our doubts. There are many birds flying in the woods, which means that there are enemies in the ambush; the beasts are panicking and fleeing, which means that they are frightened by the enemy's ambush!

The dust in the air is flying high and showing a sharp shape, which means that the enemy sent chariots to come; the dust is flying low and showing a wide shape, which means that the enemy sent the infantry to come; the dust was scattered, streaked, and far apart, it means that the enemy is gathering firewood; the dust shows a small amount and there are traces of exchanges, which means that the enemy is doing camping!

On the one hand, the enemy humbles his words, but on the one hand, he Increases defense measures. This is actually trying to attack us; on the one hand, the enemy is arrogant and drives the army forward, which is actually wanting to retreat!

The enemy first sent light chariots to the side, which was intended to form an array.

The enemy has no agreement with us and the enemy came to ask for peace, this is intended to use strategies.

The enemy is running about to reorganize the formation, which is to set the time of the attack with the soldiers. The enemy only allows half of the troops to move forward. This is to lure our attack!

In the enemy's camp, the soldiers stood leaning on weapons, because they were hungry.

The enemy engineers who were in charge of getting water from the well drank first because they were all thirsty.

The enemy sees the benefits and does not move forward to fight, because they are tired.

Many birds gathered in the enemy camp, which means that the camp is empty.

The soldiers shouted in the middle of the night because of fear.

The riots in the army are due to the fact that the general is not respected.

In the array, the flags are waving, which is due to the disorder of the army.

The officers are angry at will, this is because they feel tired.

When soldiers kill horses and eat horse meat, it means the army has run out of food. There are no water-fetching machines in the camps, and the soldiers do not go back to their dormitories to rest. This is a desperate army.

The general's attitude is sincere, the patient repeatedly exhorts the soldiers, the attitude is restrained and appear to have no authority, with a slow tone to talk to people. This is the performance of his loss of support!

The general has repeatedly rewarded the soldiers because he has encountered an embarrassing situation; the general has repeatedly punished the soldiers because he has encountered difficulties.

The general treated the soldiers fiercely first but later feared his soldiers. This is not a shrewd performance!

The enemy lowered their posture and came to confess their sins, which is to gain time and rest.

The enemy, full of anger, came to meet our army, but the two sides held each other for a long time, and the enemy neither attacked nor led the soldiers to leave. Generals must be careful to observe such unusual phenomena. (to avoid unexpected accidents!)

The army is not the more beneficial, only the general not rashly into, and enough to reunite the force, to measure the enemy's intentions and state, and then captured the enemy, this is a useful force ah! Those who do not guard and despise the enemy will become the enemy's prisoners!

If the soldiers have not been closed to the general, and the general punished them. Then they will not be convinced. If the soldiers are not convinced, it will be difficult to use! The soldiers are close to the general, but the punishment cannot be executed, then they are not available!

Therefore, the use of virtue to make the soldiers united, the use of force to make the soldiers abide by discipline, such soldiers are called soldiers who are sure to win.

The general can teach his soldiers with strict enforcement of laws and regulations, and then the soldiers will be convinced; the general cannot teach his soldiers with strict enforcement of laws, then the soldiers will not be convinced. The laws can be strictly enforced at ordinary times, this is the performance that the general has won the support of the soldiers!

Terrain

Sun Tzu said:

There are several forms of terrain: " Intercourse form", "Hanging form", "Sustaining form", " Narrow form", "Dangerous form", and "Far form".

The terrain where we can go and the enemy can come is called " Intercourse form". In the " Intercourse form ", we should first occupy the high ground and the land with sunshine, and facilitate the grain road, which is beneficial to combat.

The terrain where we can go but is difficult to return to is called "Hanging form". In the "Hanging form", if the enemy is not alert, then our side can win by attacking; if the enemy is on alert, but our side can't win by attacking, then because our side is difficult to return, it is not good for our side.

The terrain where our attack is unfavorable and the enemy's attack is also unfavorable is called a "Sustaining form". In the " Sustaining form", although the enemy let us profit, we should not attack. It is to our advantage to lure the enemy away from the terrain where he is, and not to attack him until he is halfway out of the terrain.

In "Narrow form", we should occupy this terrain first, and we must fill our soldiers with "Narrow form" to wait for the enemy to come; if the enemy occupies this terrain first, assuming that his soldiers are already filled with "Narrow form ", he cannot be pursued, and if he is not filled, he can be pursued.

In the "Dangerous form", we should first occupy this terrain, and must occupy the high ground to wait for the enemy; if the enemy occupies this terrain first, we should lure the enemy away from the terrain where he stays, and do not directly pursue him.

In the "Far form", the enemy and ourselves are too equal to challenge, to the disadvantage of those who attack first.

All these six things are the laws of the terrain; learning these laws is also an extremely important responsibility for generals, and they must be studied clearly!

In addition, the army itself has several states of failure: there is a "dash" state, a "loose" state, a "trap" state, a "collapse" state, a "chaotic" state, and an "escape" state. The formation of these six states is not a disaster caused by God, but a fault caused by generals!

When the enemy and ourselves are evenly matched, we use a troop to attack the enemy ten troops, this is called the "dash" state.

The soldiers are strong and the officials are weak. This is called the state of " loose ".

The officials are arrogant and the soldiers are cowardly. This is called the state of "trap".

Senior officers are angry and disobedient to the general. When encountering enemies, they fight against the enemy without permission. The general will not know their ability. This is called the state of "collapse."

The general is weak and not strict, and the teaching decree is not clear enough; the officials and the soldiers run or stop, and the formation of the army is disorder. This is called a "chaotic" state.

The general cannot measure the intention and state of the enemy and attacks the majority of the enemy with a few troops, and the tough enemy with weak soldiers. The army has not selected elite forward troops. This is called the "escape" state.

All these six states are the causes of failure; learning these laws is also an extremely important responsibility for generals, and they must be studied clearly!

A terrain is an auxiliary tool for the army! Measure the intention and state of the enemy to formulate a winning strategy, calculate the danger and flatness of the terrain, the advantages and disadvantages of things, the distance between far and near, this is the regulation of the superior general!

He who knows these rules and fights will surely win; He who fights without knowing these rules will surely lose.

Therefore, the general determines that our side certain to win according to the rules of war. Even if the monarch orders that he cannot fight, he can insist on fighting. The general determines that he cannot win according to the rules of war. Even if the monarch orders that he must fight, he can insist on not fighting.

Therefore, the general is attacking forward without pursuing reputation and retreats backward without avoiding guilt. The purpose is only to protect the safety of the people, and the result is also in the interest of the monarch. Then such a general is the treasure of the country!

The general treats his soldiers like babies, so he can go deep into the valley with them; The general treats his soldiers like a son, so he can fight with them to death.

The general loves the soldiers but cannot order them, treats the soldiers well but cannot command them, the soldiers' discipline is disorderly and the general cannot give the management, however; Such the soldiers are like a spoiled son, not usable!

Knowing that our soldiers can be used to attack the enemy, but not knowing that the enemy can not be attacked, such a situation is only half the chance of victory!

Knowing that the enemy can be attacked, but not knowing whether our soldiers can be used to attack the enemy, this situation is only half the chance of victory!

Knowing that the enemy can be attacked, knowing that our soldiers can be used to attack the enemy, but not knowing that the terrain can not be used for combat, such a situation is only half the chance of victory!

Therefore, those who know the laws of war act without being trapped and send troops without fail.

Therefore, in the war, those who understand the enemy and themselves, there is no danger when they win; those who understand meteorology and the function of the terrain, they can protect themselves when they win.

Nine situations of terrain

Sun Tzu said:

The so-called ancient masters who are good at fighting. They can make the enemy front and rear forces can not support each other, the number of a large and small team can not rescue each other, nobles and people can not support each other, the superiors and the inferiors can not save each other.

They can separate the enemy's soldiers and let the soldiers can not be assembled.

They can make that even if the enemy's forces assembled, his army will be out of order.

These masters weighed the situation and acted in accordance with the interests of the military, and stopped violently if they did not.

Take the liberty to ask: " the enemy is numerous and orderly, and is about to arrive, how to deal with him?" The answer was: "First seize what the enemy loves, then the enemy will be manipulated by us.

One of the most important qualities of the army is speed, which is particularly manifested in three things: launching offensives when enemy supply is difficult, walking on a path the enemy did not expect, and attacking places where the enemy is not alert! "

As long as the rules of the attacking party: going deep into the enemy's territory will unite the soldiers spontaneously, then the defending party will have difficulty defeating him; plundering the enemy's food on the rich field, then the food of the three armed forces will be sufficient. The general should be cautious in raising the strength of the soldiers without letting them get tired so that they can gather their energy and accumulate their strength; at the same time, using the army and design strategies should make people feel unpredictable. In this way, even if the general throws his army to a place where there is no way to go, the soldiers will not betray even if they die. So where can they not work themselves to the bone for the general? And the soldiers will do their best!

Soldiers will not feel fear if they fall too deep. If there is no place to go, the defense will be stable. Soldiers will be restrained when they go deep into the enemy's territory. If there is no place to go, they will naturally fight hard.

Therefore, on the offensive side, his soldiers can achieve alertness automatically without commanding them to prepare for defense, automatically support the general without asking them, automatically get close to each other without restraining them, and spontaneously without giving orders to them. In such a state, as long as the generals prohibit the words of superstition in the army and remove the things that cause the soldiers to doubt, then the soldiers will not leave the general until death!

Our soldiers do not spare money, not because they hate wealth; don't hesitate to die, not because they hate life!

On the day the order was issued, the soldiers sat with their tears on their shirts and lay with their tears on their faces.

However, the general can put them in a place where there is no way to go, and they are able to bear the pressure because they have the courage of the Cao Kui[7] and Zhuan Zhu[8]!

---

[7] Cao Kui, a native of Lu, served in Lu Zhuang Gong (reigned from 693 BC to 662 BC), was conferred as a general by Lu Zhuang Gong, and hijacked Qi Huan Gong (reigned from 685 BC to 643 BC) in the League of Ke. Cao Kui successfully asked Qi Huan Gong to return to the land he had violated and returned to his seat without changing his face afterward. Cao Kui and Zhuan Zhu were extremely brave people, and they were exemplary figures representing "courage" at that time, so Sun Tzu's cite them here to visualize the level of the courage of the soldiers.

[8] Zhuan Zhu, a native of Wu. He was an assassin hired by king Helu of Wu to kill the king Liu of Wu with a sharp dagger and finally died

Therefore, the person who is good at using the army, his way of using the army is like "Wei Ran"[9]. The so-called "Wei Ran" is the name of a snake on mount Heng[10]! When attacking its head, its tail will rescue, when attacking its tail, its head will rescue, and when attacking its waist, its head and tail will rescue.

Take the liberty to ask: "Can an army of people who hate each other make them like 'Wei Ran'?" The answer is: "Yes. This situation is like the people of the state of Vie[11] and the people of the state of Wu[12] hate each other! But when they cross the river together in a boat (in case of sudden danger), they will save each other as if they are saving their own hands. "

So even if the army is ordered to tie up the horses and bury the chariot to a depth of the whole wheel. If the general tried to use this method to keep the soldiers on the defensive, it is not enough to rely on. Let the order and courage of the soldiers seem to be from the same person. This is the effect of managing the army.

a glorious death. Therefore, king Helu of Wu was able to succeed to the throne of Wu.

[9] "Wei Ran", the original meaning of the name in ancient Chinese has a model of defense. It is Sun Tzu's metaphor for a person who is good at using the army, the state he should reach.

[10] Mountain name, a famous mountain close to Qi country.

[11] Vie: the hostile state of Wu, perished in 473 BC. The state of Vie flourished in the reign of Goujian (496-464 BC). Gou Jian, the king of Vie, took the place of Wu and became the overlord of the world.

[12] Wu: the country where Sun Tzu served, perished in 473 BC. Wu began to become powerful when the king Helu of Wu (reigned from 514 to 496 BC), appointed Sun Tzu as general and Wu Zixu as prime minister, and finally took the capital of Chu and became the world's overlord. Wu was finally destroyed by Goujian, the king of Vie, when Fuchai, the son of Helu, the king of Wu, reigned from 495 BC to 473 BC.

Both strong and weak soldiers can be used. This is the effect of using the terrain.

Therefore, a master who is good at using troops. When he uses the army, he can let the soldiers work together. It is as if he is just directing one person. This effect is actually produced by the soldiers in the state of necessity!

The task of the commanding army is to make the army quiet, deep and orderly. The general should be able to fool the soldiers ' ears and eyes so that they have no access to information to avoid a bad reaction; the general should be able to change his affairs and change his strategy so that the soldiers cannot understand and cannot catch the rules; The general should be able to change his station and march around a long winding road so that the soldiers could not think much to avoid making military operations unpredictable.

The general had to wait until he led all the troops to a high place before removing the ladder for ascending; the general had to lead all the troops deep into the territory of the vassals before releasing the relevant news. This situation is like driving the flock of sheep, driving the flock of sheep to go and driving the flock of sheep to come, but the sheep don't know where they are going!

Bringing together so many people from the three armed forces and throwing them to a dangerous place is what the commanding army will do! As for the ways of adapting to the nine types of terrain, the benefits of yielding and stretching, and the laws of the emotional response of the human heart, these are all generals must study clearly!

Any rule that acts as an attacking party: Deep into the enemy's territory will make the soldiers unite, shallow into the enemy's territory will make the soldiers loose.

When the army leaves the country and crosses the enemy's border to fight. This is called being in the "lonely terrain".

The army is in the area where it can go to other places from four directions, which is called being in the "meeting terrain".

When the army goes deep into the enemy's territory, it is called being in the "heavy terrain";

When the army goes shallow into the enemy's territory, it is called being in the "light terrain";

The army with its back to solid terrain and its front to narrow terrain is called being in the " enclosed terrain".

The army with its back to solid terrain and its front to the enemy is called being in the "dead terrain".

The army has no way to go. This is called being in the "poor terrain."

Therefore, in the "scattered terrain", I will try to make the soldiers single-minded.

In the "light terrain", I will make the army leave quickly.

In the "competing terrain", I will keep the army from staying.

In the "intersecting terrain", I will stick to the point of advancing and retreating.

In the "meeting terrain", I will treat diplomatic countries near the area with caution

In the "heavy terrain", I will let the rear troops step up their pace.

In the "covered terrain", I will let the army continue to move forward without stopping.

In the "enclosed terrain", I will block all escape gaps by myself.

In the "dead terrain", I will let the soldiers fully understand that there is no other chance of survival but to kill the enemy and win.

The vassals' basic response to the war was to defend the enemy as soon as he came, to fight as soon as he had to, and to pursue him as soon as he passed through our territory.

Therefore, if you do not know the plots of the vassals, you cannot associate with them in advance; you cannot march if you do not know the terrain such as mountains, forests, obstacles, and rivers; you cannot get geographical advantages without using the locals as a guide.

There is one thing that the general does not know about these four or five things. He is not leading the army of kings and hegemons!

The armies of kings and hegemons: When they are fighting against a big country, they can prevent the enemy's army from gathering; when they exert force to the enemy, they can prevent the enemy assembles his Allies.

Therefore, those monarchs who do not maintain diplomatic relations with the vassals of the world, do not serve the vassals who have the authority of the world; only want to pursue their own desires and exert force to the enemy; then their castles are likely to be captured, and their country is in danger of being destroyed!

When the army is fighting abroad, the generals sometimes have to carry out rewards that are not stipulated in the statutory provisions, and orders that have not been approved and issued by the government.

It is as easy to command so many men of the three armies to break through the enemy's encirclement as to command one man: to command the soldiers to break through the encirclement by concrete facts, not by illusory words; command the soldiers to break through are made by telling soldiers what kind of harm can be eliminated by doing so, rather than telling them what benefits they will get by doing so.

The general put the soldiers where they might be destroyed at any time, but the soldiers could survive; the general put the soldiers in a situation where they could face death at any time, but the soldiers could survive.

When everyone in the army is trapped in a dangerous situation together, they can realize their potential and fight hard, and the general will have the chance to win in defeat. Therefore, the task of using the army is to carefully understand the enemy's intention, to concentrate all the forces in this direction, so that we can successfully kill the enemy's generals even if we go to the battlefield thousands of miles away. This method is called "smart things."

Therefore, on the day when the decree decided to wage war against the enemy, the envoys who stayed in the country could not be given the opportunity to go back and report; the oath ceremony in the temple to encourage the morale of the army, establish justification for actions against the enemy by declaring the guilt of the enemy.

The enemy opened the door, we must enter as soon as possible, first attack the place the enemy cherishes, do not agree with the enemy on the date of the battle, quietly capture and attack the enemy, in order to achieve the purpose of war.

Therefore, in the beginning, we should act like a quiet maiden, let the enemy lose vigilance and open the door; then the action should be as fast as the escaped hare, making the enemy too late to resist.

Attack with fire

Sun Tzu said:

There are five main targets for using fire attack: the first is to burn people, the second is to burn piled material, the third is to burn equipment, the fourth is to burn warehouses, and the fifth is to burn the grass.

The use of fire attacks must rely on certain conditions, these conditions must always be prepared.

There is a proper time to launch a fire attack, and there are suitable days for setting fires. Time refers to when the weather is dry; day refers to the period during which the moon passes through the four stars, dustpan, wall, wing, and car; [13]When the moon moves to the

---

[13] The four constellations belonging to the twenty-eight constellations of ancient China, their names reflect their shape. Twenty-eight places are located near the ecliptic and equator on the celestial sphere and are an important part of the equatorial coordinate system in ancient astronomy. Each place contains more than one fixed star, and the fixed stars are connected to the fixed stars to form a constellation unit, each occupying a sky area. The dustpan is an oriental coordinate system, Wall is a northern coordinate system, and Wing and Car are a southern coordinate system. The dustpan contains four stars (γ Sgr, δ Sgr, ε Sgr, and η Sgr), corresponding to the modern Sagittarius. The wall contains two stars (γ Peg, α And), corresponds to modern Pegasus and Andromeda. The wing contains four stars (γ Crv, ε Crv, δ Crv, and β Crv), corresponds to the modern Crater and Hydra. The car contains four stars (γ Crv, ε Crv, δ Crv, β Crv), corresponding to the modern Corvus. People in the Spring and Autumn Period are already very good at using changes in constellation operations to predict things like weather and earthquakes. For example, Confucius once used the "Book of Songs" to record "The moon is separated from the Net, it will rain heavily." The Net is one of the twenty-eight constellations. It successfully predicted rain and was regarded as a saint. Yan Tzu also used the changes in constellation operation to successfully predict an

positions of the four stars, it is usually the day when the wind begins to blow.

When using a fire attack, be sure to take corresponding actions based on the changes in the five possible developments. These five possible developments refer to:

(1) If a fire attack is launched from inside the enemy, the army will launch an attack outside as a response.

(2) When a fire attack is launched, but the enemy is very quiet, then do not attack them. When the fire has reached its limit, chase them if they can be chased, and stop if they can't be chased.

(3) If a fire attack can be launched from the outside of the enemy, so don't wait to launch from the inside of the enemy. Use the timing to decide when to fire.

(4) Do not attack enemies in the leeward when the fire attack is launched in the windward.

(5) If the wind blows long in the day, it tends to stop at night.

All commanders of the army must know the changes of these five kinds of fire and follow the rules to take advantage of them.

So generals who use fire to assist their attacks are "smart" and those who use water to assist their attacks are "strong". Water attack can be used to block the enemy, but not to seize his goods.

---

earthquake. Sun Tzu said that the same method cited by Confucius used the movement of the moon relative to the constellations, such as traveling to or leaving a certain constellation, to predict the weather and meteorology. According to empirical statistics, the ancients learned that when the moon passed these four places, the winds were the most frequent. Therefore, in order to achieve the best results of attack with fire, Sun Tzu also incorporated such statistical data based on the rule of thumb into the system of fire attacks. His concept is advanced.

After winning the battle and capturing the castle, the general does not practice moral politics, then there is danger! The monarch should order the general: Don't stay.

Therefore, a wise monarch and a good general should seriously consider and be vigilant in the following matters. Do not wage war without interests, do not use the army without gaining popular support, and do not actively seek fighting without encountering danger.

The monarch cannot wage war because of anger, the general cannot fight because of fury. We can do only if it is in the interests of the country, if not then we stop.

Anger can return to a state of pleasure, fury can return to a state of joy, but a perished country cannot return to the state of existence, and a dead man cannot return to the state of living!

So for these things, the wise monarch must be cautious, and the good general must be vigilant. This is the way to stabilize the country!

Using Spies

Sun Tzu said:

Launching an army of 100,000 troops, mobilizing thousands of miles away, the people's expenses and the public's expenses will use thousands of gold every day.

As a result, there was turmoil at home and abroad, and the people were tired of being on the road to the expedition. Therefore, there were as many as seven hundred thousand families who were unable to continue their own businesses.

Soldiers and their family members have to wait for a reunion for many years, just because the monarch needs them to win the war. However, the superiors did not know the enemy's situation because they cherished the title of nobility, income, and money. This is the ultimate of unkindness! This is not the general of the people! This is not the assistant of the monarch! This is not the master of victory!

Wise monarch and capable general can defeat their enemies once they take action, and the success is far above everyone: this is because they know the enemy's situation in advance.

To know the enemy's situation in advance, can't get it from ghosts and gods, can't draw it from the past examples, can't get it from guessing, must get it from someone who knows the enemy 's situation!

If the monarch wants to deploy spies, there are five types of spies available for him: Native Spies, Official Spies, Traitorous Spies, Dead Spies, and Alive Spies. The monarch should use these five types of spies simultaneously, making enemies confused about the rules of his spy deployment. This is called the Magic Rule, which is the monarch's treasure!

The so-called Native Spies refer to the enemy country's natives who are used as our spies; Official Spies refer to the enemy country's officials who are used as our spies; Traitorous Spies refer to the enemy country's spies who are used as our spies; Dead Spies refer to spies who are likely to die because of sending false information to enemies and convincing enemies of it at the cost of their lives, and Alive Spies refer to spies who can come back alive and report the information about enemies.

Therefore, in the army, no other person is closer to the general than spies; no other person gets more rewards from the general than spies, and no other person discusses more confidential issues with the general than spies.

If a general is not wise enough, he cannot make use of spies very well; if a general is not benevolent enough, he cannot manipulate spies very well; if a general is not secretive enough, he cannot comprehend true intentions of spies.

Be secretive! Be secretive! Spies can be used everywhere!

Before a military operation plotted with spies takes place, those who are informed of this operation and those who inform others of this operation should all be executed.

We must acquire information about all troops that we want to attack, all castles we want to occupy and all enemies we want to kill, including names of their generals, capable assistants to these generals, their officials who receive guests, their doorkeepers and their guests. Make sure that our spies can capture the enemy country's spies who sneak into our troops. We should lure them to betray their country with interests and set them free. Like this, we can make them to be our Traitorous Spies and put them to use.

With the Traitorous Spies working in the enemy's camp, we can get some Native Spies and Official Spies and make use of them; With the Traitorous Spies working in the enemy's camp, we can dispatch Dead Spies to spread false information to enemies; and with the Traitorous Spies working in the enemy's camp, our Alive Spies can successfully bring back information on schedule!

Monarchs and generals must know these five types of spies. More importantly, they must know that the key is Traitorous Spies. So, make sure to treat Traitorous Spies kindly and generously!

The rise of the Shang Dynasty was due to Yi Yin[14] being a spy in the Xia Dynasty, and the rise of the Zhou Dynasty was due to Jiang Taigong[15] being a spy in the Shang Dynasty.

If wise monarchs and capable generals who can use people of great wisdom as spies, they will make a great success. This is not only the key to war but also the basis for all military plans and operations!

---

[14] Yi Yin was a founding hero of the Shang Dynasty. He served as a spy for King Tang of the Shang Dynasty, went to the court of the King of the Xia Dynasty as an official, and carried out intelligence collection and subversion. Yi Yin owed much credit to the demise of the Xia Dynasty. Therefore, after the fall of the Xia Dynasty, Yi Yin became the prime minister of the Shang Dynasty. After Tang's death, Yi Yin once banished the faint Shang Dynasty king Taijia and did not return the throne to him until Taijia improved. He Is a very wise person.

[15] Jiang Taigong was the founding hero of the Zhou Dynasty. He assisted King Wen and King Wu, and served as a spy for King Wen. He entered the court of King Shang for intelligence collection and subversion. In the end, because of the great merits, he was sealed in Qi State and became the founding father of Qi State. It is said that he was the writer of the "Six Taos", and he had a great effect and influence on the formation of the military culture of Qi State and the customs of Qi State. He was a very wise elder at the time.

www.ingramcontent.com/pod-product-compliance
Lightning Source LLC
Chambersburg PA
CBHW030531220526
45463CB00007B/2783